LILLIAN TOO'S
Little Book of
CREATING
ABUNDANCE

D0259935

RIDER

LONDON · SYDNEY · AUCKLAND · JOHANNESBURG

Extracted from Lillian Too's Creating Abundance With Feng Shui.
First published in 2000 by Rider, an imprint of Ebury Press
Random House, 20 Vauxhall Bridge Road, London SW1V 2SA
www.randomhouse.co.uk

Random House Australia (Pty) Limited
20 Alfred Street, Milsons Point, Sydney,
New South Wales 2061, Australia

Random House New Zealand Limited
18 Poland Road, Glenfield, Auckland 10, New Zealand

Random House South Africa (Pty) Limited
Endulini, 5A Jubilee Road, Parktown 2193, South Africa

The Random House Group Limited Reg. No. 954009

Papers used by Rider are natural, recyclable products made from
wood grown in sustainable forests.

Printed and bound in Denmark by Nørhaven A/S, Viborg

A CIP catalogue record for this book is available from the
British Library

ISBN 0-7126-0065-5

Contents

A Wealth of Abundance   5

Location   19

Understanding Chi   24

Understanding the Five Elements   32

Delineating and Defining Your Space   36

Combining Earth Luck With

   Mankind Luck   47

An Abundance of Personal Growth   50

An Abundance of Acclaim   60

An Abundance of Success   77

An Abundance of Good Health   109

An Abundance of Love   120

An Abundance of Good Family Luck   131

An Abundance of Material Possessions   147

An Abundance of Happiness   153

A WEALTH OF ABUNDANCE

•

MORE THAN MONEY ...

Creating abundance is more than just
making money. Abundance embraces
all the wonderful things that deepen
and expand one's life.

THE EIGHT KINDS OF ABUNDANCE

An abundance of material possessions,
of recognition, success, good health,
loving relationships, good family life,
personal growth and happiness are the
different manifestations of abundance
which make life meaningful.

ATTRACTING ABUNDANCE

Combining the best of feng shui
practice with the power of your mind
creates an overflow of auspicious
cosmic chi which in turn attracts
abundance of various kinds – wealth,
prosperity, health, acclaim, popularity,
happiness and simply feeling good
about yourself.

CLARIFYING YOUR ASPIRATIONS

If you want success, identify the kind
of success you want. Do the same for
relationships. Feng shui has the
potential to enhance and actualize all
your aspirations. Thinking them
through helps to make them happen the
way you want them to.

BE COMFORTABLE ABOUT
WANTING ABUNDANCE

Until you have thought deeply about
abundance and feel comfortable about
wanting it in your life, it will be
difficult to attract the manifestations of
abundance. To successfully create
abundance you must want it with a
passion, but not obsession.

IT'S OKAY TO BE SCEPTICAL

It is perfectly natural to react with a healthy dose of scepticism to the idea that by living in accordance with feng shui you will actualize all the ingredients of abundance into your life. Don't let that stop you from experimentation. You have nothing to lose!

BELIEVE IN YOURSELF

Feng shui brings positive results when
practised correctly. But once you have
decided to apply feng shui to improve
and enhance your living space, it is
more important to believe in yourself
and have confidence that you are doing
it right than to believe in feng shui.

THE PHILOSOPHY OF
THE I CHING

Feng shui has been influenced
enormously by the philosophy of the
Chinese classic known as the I Ching,
which states that everything is in a
state of flux, constantly changing and
evolving. Good fortune accordingly
transmutes into misfortune, and back
again, in a rhythmic cycle.

THE CYCLE OF GOOD AND BAD LUCK

Feng shui seeks to understand the earth's energies and develop ways to manipulate them. Through the correct use of feng shui, periods of bad luck can be modified so that misfortunes are minimized, and periods of good luck enhanced so that good fortune is multiplied.

HOW FENG SHUI WORKS

While feng shui is the science of
space, it is also a reflection of the
mind. It actualizes on the physical and
material plane all that the mind
associates with the symbols that are
used in the practice of feng shui.

KEEP AN OPEN MIND

When you are open and receptive to feng shui's many methods of drawing an abundance of wealth and good health into your life, your own personal energies will start to help you formulate the ideal way to create and arrange your space.

LIMITLESS ABUNDANCE

Feng shui has the potential to fulfil our
wishes and aspirations on various
levels, and when combined with the
power of the fully awakened mind,
there is no limit to the great good
fortune it can bring into our lives.

VISUALIZED FENG SHUI IS VERY POTENT

By studying feng shui techniques and understanding the symbolism involved, then visualizing the relevant feng shui enhancer or energizer working powerfully wherever it has been placed, you will combine feng shui with the mind's vast potential to actualize dreams and aspirations.

NOTHING IS FENG SHUI PERFECT

Adapt feng shui to your own particular circumstances and remember it is almost impossible to achieve perfect feng shui. Every house has its share of wrong corners, inauspiciously shaped rooms and so on. Don't panic! Creative solutions can be found for almost everything.

LOCATION

•

GREEN DRAGON

This is one of four celestial animals
fundamental to feng shui and the
search for an auspicious site. The
dragon is epitomized by gently
undulating hills and lies to the east, or
to the left of your main door.

WHITE TIGER

The white tiger of the west, or to the
right of your main door, exudes
protective energies that enhance the
presence of the green dragon. Where
the dragon resides, the tiger is also
said to be present and need not,
therefore, be activated inside the
home. The tiger protects the home.

DRAGON HILLS

Classic feng shui regards places where
the green dragon lives as highly
auspicious locations. Dragon hills are
lush and verdant, the air smells good
and gentle breezes blow. Shade and
sunlight reflect the balance of
yin and yang.

MODERN LANDSCAPES

According to the principles of
landscape feng shui as it is practised
today, buildings are deemed to
represent dragons and tigers, while
roads are viewed in the same way as
the waterways of olden days. Thus the
auspicious green dragon/white tiger can
be created artificially.

THE IDEAL ENVIRONMENT

The land to the east of your house, or
on the left of your front door, should be
higher than that to the west, or right.
Land behind your house should be
higher than that in front, which should
be flat and empty to allow good chi to
settle and accumulate.

UNDERSTANDING CHI

•

CHI – THE COSMIC BREATH

Central to the understanding of feng
shui is the concept of the cosmic
breath of the celestial dragon. This
breath, referred to as the chi of the
environment, is said to be the life
force, or energy, that pervades man's
existence.

BENEFICIAL AND
HARMFUL CHI

When the energies of any space are in
harmony, the cosmic breath of that
space is auspicious. This beneficial
breath is termed sheng chi. However
when chi travels too fast, and when it
becomes stagnant, it becomes harmful.
This killing breath is called shar chi.

THE ESSENCE OF GOOD
FENG SHUI

The purpose of feng shui is to trap the
cosmic breath flowing through a site
and create an environment in which it
can accumulate without becoming
stagnant. In such an environment
wealth, prosperity and abundance will
flourish and grow.

HARNESSING THE
DRAGON'S BREATH

Waterways and roads should be slow
and meandering rather than straight,
and sites should be protected from
harsh winds. Chi tends to stop and
accumulate when bounded by water, so
the presence of water is usually
auspicious. But not when the water is
polluted or fast flowing.

POISON ARROWS AND THE KILLING BREATH

Feng shui warns against inauspicious energy, known as shar chi or the killing breath, which is caused by the presence of secret poison arrows. Poison arrows are created by pointed, angled and sharp objects that seem to be aimed directly at a house, and especially its main door.

EXAMPLES OF POISON
ARROWS

Straight roads, rivers or railway lines
that seem to be aimed directly at the
main front door, triangular shaped roof
lines caused by neighbours homes, and
the sharp edges of large buildings all
emit strong poison arrows that can
cause severe bad luck.

DEFLECTING POISON ARROWS

There is always a solution to the problem of poison arrows, which can be deflected, dissolved or diffused by changing the position or direction of your main door, planting trees and building walls.

MIRRORS

A very convenient solution to poison arrows emitted from a structure and directed towards your front door is to use a mirror to reflect back the bad flow of energy. However as this can harm your neighbours it is preferable to find alternative cures.

UNDERSTANDING THE FIVE ELEMENTS

•

THE LUCK OF THE EARTH

Feng shui is the luck of the earth, and when we use feng shui we are tapping into the earth's auspicious energies. Earth is one of five elements, and the way they interact in any space is what creates good or bad luck.

THE FIVE ELEMENTS

Every object, circumstance, direction,
season and so on represents one of the
five elements – water, wood, fire, earth
and metal. Element analysis and an
understanding of the cycles of the
elements is central to the practice
of feng shui.

THE PRODUCTIVE CYCLE

In this cycle, water produces wood which produces fire which produces earth which produces metal which produces water. Elements are compatible and harmonious when one produces the other. Thus green and brown, which suggest wood, are complemented by blue or black, the colours of water.

THE DESTRUCTIVE CYCLE

In this cycle fire destroys metal which
destroys wood which destroys earth
which destroys water which destroys
fire. Elements are incompatible when
one destroys another. If you decorate
your living room in red and blue the
elements are clashing because water
destroys fire.

DELINEATING AND DEFINING YOUR SPACE

•

DETERMINE THE DIRECTION OF YOUR MAIN DOOR

The direction that your main door faces is regarded as the front of your house, and ideally the front of your house should be facing the nearest main road that lies in the vicinity of your home.

FIND THE CENTRE AND THE EIGHT COMPASS DIRECTIONS

After determining the door direction, the next thing is to determine the door location by dividing a layout plan of your home into a grid of nine equal squares or rectangles. Notice if you have any missing or protruding corners.

THE PA KUA

This is an eight-sided symbol of feng shui on each side of which is one of eight trigrams, each having a range of symbolic meanings and associated elements, numbers and qualities, and correlating with one of the eight compass directions.

THE SOUTH

The south belongs to the element
of fire. It is a very yang direction
associated with various shades of red,
or very bright yellow. Displaying a
phoenix in the south brings enormous
good fortune which manifests in many
beneficial opportunities coming
your way.

THE NORTH

This corner belongs to the water
element. It is very yin and the
dominant colour is black. Blues and
deep purples are very auspicious here.
Displaying a tortoise in the north
brings great good fortune for the
whole family.

THE EAST

Here the element is wood and this is
the best place in the house for the
eldest son, or for an only child of either
sex, because the east signifies growth.
The east is also the place of the
auspicious green dragon. To enhance
east corners use plenty of lush
verdant plants.

THE WEST

This can be a place of joy, where gold can be found. It belongs to the metal element and its dominant colour is white. It is the place of the white tiger, although one should avoid displaying this creature here since mainly people born in the years of the tiger or dragon can sustain its powerful energies.

THE SOUTHEAST

The element of this corner, which symbolizes the wind of feng shui, is small wood. It is the corner usually associated with wealth and is energized with plants and flowers. Lights are also excellent. When all five elements are present, wood grows at its most efficient and fastest. This signifies good tidings.

THE SOUTHWEST

The element of this corner, the place of
the matriarch and focal point for
relationships, is big earth. When this
corner is missing or afflicted with the
presence of a toilet or storeroom, all
residents suffer. When all elements are
present, earth energies are at their
most potent.

NORTHEAST

This place is usually associated with a time of preparation – the mountain. Here the element is earth. Placing a wealth vase here is symbolic of gold inside the mountain. Place the vase inside a cupboard in this corner to ensure that the luck of the family will get better with the passing of time.

THE NORTHWEST

The northwest is the place of the patriarch or breadwinner and its element is big metal. Like the southwest, it is a vital corner of the house and if adversely affected by having a toilet placed there the fortunes of the patriarch will suffer. The best colours here are metallic or white.

COMBINING EARTH LUCK WITH MANKIND LUCK

•

THE TRINITY OF LUCK

Feng shui is only one third in the trinity of luck – heaven luck, earth luck and mankind luck. Heaven luck, or destiny, is out of our control. But we can improve our earth luck through the practice of feng shui and our mankind luck through our own attitudes and mind sets.

TAKE ADVANTAGE OF
OPPORTUNITIES

Creating good feng shui in your living
space paves the way for wonderful
opportunities to come into your life –
new people, new situations, new
developments. But all these will come
to nought if you do not grasp the
opportunities they afford to transform
your life.

PURIFYING YOUR LIVING SPACE

Every house will benefit from having
the energies inside the home swept
clean of lingering stagnant energy.
Once a week open all windows and
turn on all fans for about an hour to
allow the energy inside the house to be
refreshed by outside air flowing in.

AN ABUNDANCE OF PERSONAL GROWTH

•

BECOME A WINNER

Winning is an attitude and a mind set.
But winning also requires luck: being
in the right place at the right time,
having opportunities come your way.
Feng shui can provide this bit of luck
to give you the necessary boost to tip
results in your favour.

ACCEPT YOURSELF
AS YOU ARE

To make the best use of feng shui, you
must start by seeing real value in
yourself. You must accept yourself and
your life situation unconditionally.
Embrace the person you are and
discard feelings of unworthiness
and inferiority.

TUNE IN TO YOUR OWN FORCE FIELD

Standing with your feet hip width apart,
bend your knees slightly and lower
your body keeping your back straight.
Bring your hands in front of you, palms
facing, and gently move them towards
one another then slightly apart. Tune in
and feel your palms heat up. Feel the
energy, or chi, between them.

ENERGIZING QUARTZ CRYSTAL FOR GOOD LUCK

Warm your hands as described previously. Place them around a piece of quartz crystal or a crystal ball then put the crystal on a table in the northeast corner of your living room or study. This will bring powerful earth luck to your efforts to improve yourself.

USING CRYSTAL TO IMPROVE EDUCATIONAL AND EXAM RESULTS

Let each child have his or her own crystal and energize it as described above. Place the crystal on a table in the northeast of the living room or his or her bedroom. This works by making children more focused, improving their concentration and making them highly motivated.

A GLOBE

An even more effective way to energize education luck is to place a real globe – ultimate symbol of the earth – in the northeast corner. This may be a globe of the earth rotating on its axis or, better still, one made of crystal, lapis lazuli or topaz. Let the child energize the globe as before.

FORCES CREATED BY
PHYSICAL OBJECTS

These kinds of blockages are the
easiest to deal with since physical
objects can be moved and rearranged
to allow energies to flow in a
harmonious and auspicious way. The
rule of thumb is that energy should be
made to flow slowly, in a gently
curving way.

THE FREE FLOW OF
MOVEMENT

Let the flow of movement within the
home stay clear of protruding sharp
corners and heavy, exposed, overhead
beams. If a pillar is blocking the flow,
softens its edges with plants or wrap it
with mirrors to symbolically make it
disappear.

CLEAR THE CLUTTER

If there is too much clutter blocking
the flow of chi, clear it. If there is too
much furniture give some away. Throw
out old papers, bags, worn out clothes
and all the baggage we all tend to
collect. Let the flow of the home be
smooth at all times.

GOOD MAINTENANCE IS
GOOD FENG SHUI

When drains get blocked, repair them.
When bulbs have blown, change them.
When furniture seems wobbly and the
hinges spoilt, get them all repaired as
soon as you can. When everything
works the feng shui is smooth.

AN ABUNDANCE OF ACCLAIM

•

A GOOD NAME

According to Chinese tradition, life is
devoid of meaning if you do not have a
good name. A vital goal of feng shui is
therefore to activate abundance in the
form of a reputation that is honourable
and highly respected, without which
other forms of success are difficult
to realize.

RECOGNITION IS A
PREREQUISITE OF SUCCESS

What differentiates the very successful
from other equally or even more
talented and hard working but less
successful people is the luck of
recognition. Winners harness mankind
luck by their determination to succeed
and earth luck through good feng shui.

YIN AND YANG

Yin and yang are opposite, but
complementary, poles of the cosmic
spectrum of experience. Yin is dark,
and symbolizes inactivity and death,
while yang signifies brightness, activity
and growth, and all that is abundant
and energetic about life. Although
opposites they give life to one another.

A YANG LIFE

Having a yang life suggest a life of
great abundance, and houses of the
living are described as yang houses.
The Chinese refer to hugely successful
individuals as those who enjoy the
great abundance of having a very yang
life.

BALANCING YIN AND YANG

Good feng shui creates an optimum
balance of yin and yang which, in the
houses of the living, suggests the need
for a greater dose of yang than yin. But
since yin and yang give life to one
another, yin should never be
overshadowed to an extent that it
becomes completely absent.

ACTIVATING THE LUCK OF REPUTATION

The south corner is the part of the home associated with good reputation and the most effective way to activate this kind of luck is to hang a beautiful crystal chandelier in the south. When the light is kept on for the better part of the day, it will bring fame and fortune too, and benefit all residents.

PAINT IT RED

Another way to energize the luck of reputation is to paint the south part of the house a very bright red, a powerful yang colour associated with good reputation luck. If a whole room in red sounds too much, just paint the door red.

SUNRISE AND SUNFLOWERS

Hanging a painting of a sunrise, or of
sunflowers in full bloom, in the south
also activates the luck of acclaim.
Displaying fresh flowers in the south is
also very yang but once the flowers
fade they become yin and must be
thrown out.

POOR FENG SHUI IN THE SOUTH

A south corner which is too yin or that is being hit by inauspicious shar chi causes enemies to speak ill of the family and engenders a general air of bad feeling. Excessive yin energy in the south is caused by the presence of too many water symbols, such as the colours blue and black.

COUNTERACTING SHAR CHI
WITH PLANTS

If shar chi in the south corner of a
house is caused by poison arrows
coming from the sharp edges of
protruding corners, walls or stand-
alone pillars, use fresh, healthy plants
to soften the edges of corners and
diffuse the killing energy. Change the
plants every two or three months.

COUNTERACTING SHAR CHI
WITH WIND CHIMES

Wind chimes are an effective way to
slow down the fast flow of killing chi
caused by three doors in a row or a
long corridor leading into the south
corner. Make sure you use a five-rod
wind chime for this particular purpose.

LET THERE BE LIGHT

Good lighting in the south acts as a
powerful magnet for drawing the luck
of acclaim. A well-lit home generally
has better feng shui than one that looks
dim and has diffused lighting
throughout. Do not, however, use
spotlights which are blinding, like
looking directly at the sun.

ENERGIZING FOR ACCLAIM
WITH LIGHTS

Make sure the whole of the south
corner is well lit by a well placed light,
preferably a crystal chandelier, at the
ceiling. The light reflected off the
facets of cut glass creates exactly the
right kind of energy to attract acclaim,
which is why chandeliers make such
wonderful energizers.

UPLIGHTING

Let the light seem to shine upwards to
engender a sense of upward moving
energy and make sure the ceiling in the
south corner is white as this also
creates the feeling of yang.

ENERGIZING FOR ACCLAIM
IN YOUR GARDEN

If you have a garden, it is also a good
idea to keep the south side of the
garden well lit, day and night. Pets
kept in the south represent life activity
and are excellent yang energizers.

THE YANG ENERGY OF FIRE

A fireplace located on the south wall of
the living room is most auspicious.
Apart from generating good fire
element energy during the yin winter
months, the fireplace also acts as an
energizer for attracting the luck of
recognition.

LIGHTED CANDLES

If you do not have a fireplace, make
space along the south wall for lighted
candles, which create good yang energy
that benefits the whole family. Be sure
never to leave a naked flame burning
when there is no one around.

AN ABUNDANCE OF SUCCESS

THE SPIRAL OF SUCCESS

Arranging your living space according to feng shui principles creates an aura of success which brings great abundance and produces an aura of confidence. This in turn creates a positive attitude, which brings yet more success. Success breeds success!

SEE THE BIG PICTURE

People who are achievement oriented
seldom allow small inconveniences to
irritate them and rarely breach the
harmony of energies that surrounds
them by breaking into anger. This
mental attitude is a reflection of
their inner feng shui.

INNER FENG SHUI

This is a state of mental equilibrium that comes with a calm and relaxed disposition. Meditation helps to create this disposition, as do suitable visualizations that calm the inner spirit. Success energies should be created internally as well as externally.

GENERATE POSITIVE ENERGY

This is like creating internalized feng shui and involves arranging images in your mind which place you in centre stage, benefiting from the vibrations of your personalized space. Energies created by your mind, positive or negative, are very powerful. Make strong positive statements about yourself.

AFFIRMATIONS

By using affirmations – positive
statements about yourself – to
penetrate your subconscious mind, you
will be empowering your inner success
energies even more. Affirm your belief
in yourself and your potential for
success by working affirmations into
your daily routine.

NEGATIVE BELIEFS

Over the years we amass mental
blockages caused by repressed
emotions such as fear, guilt and anger,
and by negative programming many of
us have been subjected to since
childhood. These blocks work like
killing energy and must be dissolved to
let our energies flow smoothly.

MENTAL SPRING-CLEANING

Mental spring-cleaning helps remove mental blockages and get the flow of energy moving. Start by accepting your own limiting attitudes and beliefs, and identifying the true nature of your fears. Simply focusing in this way may be sufficient to dissolve negative attitudes.

FORGIVENESS

Holding grudges and vengeful thoughts
drains you of energy, however justified
your feelings of anger or injury.
Forgiveness creates a powerful sense of
liberation. It is like unleashing a dam
of suppressed negative energies. It
really does feel better to forgive and
release yourself.

NEGATIVE ENERGIES

Success often depends on the approval,
consent or help of other people.
Everyone has their fair share of
admirers and enemies, and the
negativities being sent your way by
those who are hostile to you need to be
cleared.

LOVE YOUR ENEMIES

Send symbols of love and peace and
goodwill towards everyone who may
have reason (or not) to dislike you or
would harm you. Visualize a host of
white doves, hearts and even kisses
flowing towards your enemies from you.
Soften your own attitude towards
your enemies.

CLARIFY YOUR GOALS AND
PRIORITIZE

Do you define success in terms of
money, career, lifestyle, relationships,
leisure time, family, personal growth,
love, power, possessions, recognition,
specific achievements or having a great
and healthy body? Think through and
order your priorities and you will
achieve greater success luck with
feng shui.

THE MAIN DOOR

Probably the most important part of
your house to attend to in terms of feng
shui is your main door, the door that
you normally use to enter and leave
your house or apartment. This is where
all good fortune chi meant for your
home enters and accumulates.

ENSURE NO POISON ARROWS HIT YOUR MAIN DOOR

Roads and roof lines cause the most
harm to main doors so watch out for
them. If your main door faces a straight
road coming directly at it, hang a yin
pa kua mirror to reflect the killing chi.
Similarly the triangular pointed shape
of a neighbour's house should not hit
your main door.

THE MOUNTAIN SHOULD
BE BEHIND

Your main door should never face
higher land. If it does you should either
change the door direction or, if this is
not possible, hang a sizeable mirror to
reflect the mountain in front.

FREE ACCESS

Any furniture placed outside should
never be allowed to block your main
door. Physical impediments easily
translate into blockages in your life,
preventing you from enjoying success
in any of your endeavours.

LANES, PATHS AND DRIVEWAYS

Any lane or path leading to our main
door should be curved and preferably
winding, and of even width all the way
along. A straight path that leads
directly into your home sends slivers of
killing energy. Placing lights on the
pathway is auspicious.

THE MAIN DOOR FACING A STAIRCASE

It is inauspicious for the main door to face a staircase or a straight line of doors. Create a barrier between the doors, or the door and stairway, or hang a five-rod wind chime.

AVOID MIRRORS OPPOSITE
THE MAIN DOOR

If the main door opens to face a wall
with a mirror on it, all good fortune
coming into your home will be reflected
away again.

GOOD LIGHTING

For the main door to be auspicious it
should have good lighting both inside
and outside. When a hallway is well lit
it attracts chi.

BEDROOM FENG SHUI

If your bedroom enjoys good feng shui,
then good fortune will manifest in all
areas of your life. You will enjoy
success at work and in your outside
relationships, you will have good
health, and you will definitely have a
happy home and family life.

BED LOCATIONS

Beds should not be placed between two doors, or directly pointed towards the entrance so that the feet point towards the door. Nor should beds be located directly under windows or beneath exposed overhead beams, ceiling fans or a toilet from the floor above.

NEVER REFLECT A BED IN A MIRROR

Mirrors positioned so that they reflect the bed cause great unhappiness, and often lead to the break-up of couples due to the entrée of a third party into the marriage. Mirrors directly facing one another, so that an infinite number of reflections is created, are also highly inauspicious.

AVOID WATER FEATURES IN THE BEDROOM

A water feature in the bedroom is said to have the same negative effects as reflecting mirrors. Try to avoid water motifs in your bedroom furniture, decoration or paintings. However this does not mean that you cannot have a glass of water, small refrigerator or a jug in the bedroom.

LIVE PLANTS

Contrary to popular belief, flowers and plants in the bedroom are not auspicious. Plants represent yang energy and in other parts of the house they are excellent. In the bedroom, however, they cause sleep problems and sap one's energy.

DESIGNING AN AUSPICIOUS OFFICE

If your office is shaped irregularly try
to use plants and mirrors to regularize
it. Do not locate your office at the end
of a long corridor, next to a toilet,
especially not sharing a wall with a
toilet, nor below a toilet.

NEVER SIT WITH YOUR
BACK TO THE DOOR

This will cause you to be stabbed in the back. Never place your chair or desk in a way that you cannot see people entering the room, nor sit with the door directly in front of you.

ALWAYS HAVE SOMETHING
SOLID BEHIND YOU

Never sit with your back to the window.
Ideal is a wall behind you on which is
hung a picture of a mountain, which
will provide much needed support, a
vital ingredient of success.

EXPOSED OVERHEAD BEAMS

Sitting directly under exposed beams will impair your judgements and the decisions you make. You should also be careful not to sit in the line of fire of killing energy caused by protruding corners. Place plants strategically to dissolve such negative energies.

THE GOOD FORTUNE DESK

The dimensions for an executive desk are 152 x 89 cm (60 x 35 in). The height should be 84 cm (33 in). You can also energize the table top with feng shui, and have auspicious symbols such as dragons and tortoises carved as decorative items on the sides and drawers of your table.

THE EXECUTIVE CHAIR

This should have a high back,
completely covering your torso, to
symbolize support. A height of 109 cm
(43 in) brings prosperity luck. Your
chair should also have armrests. If it
does not, the celestial animals – the
dragon and tiger – are said to be
missing and you will lack protection
in your work.

BALANCING YIN AND YANG

Make sure your office is well lit. If it is not, yang energy is weakened. But if afternoon sun comes in, make sure it does not get too hot, as this produces excessive yang energy.

PLACE A PLANT IN THE EAST OR SOUTHEAST CORNER

An important feng shui item for the office is a live, healthy plant with lush foliage. The presence of a plant represents growth energy because the energy movement of the wood element is upwards. This is symbolically excellent for the office.

AN ABUNDANCE OF GOOD HEALTH

•

THE IMPORTANCE OF GOOD HEALTH

Good health leads to a long and healthy life and ensures that when we get sick we will recover swiftly. Good health is considered more valuable than material wealth, since without it wealth and prosperity cannot be enjoyed.

NOURISHING CHI

All traditional Chinese practices focus
on nourishing chi, both externally in
the environment as with feng shui, and
internally through meditation and
breathing exercises, chi kung,
acupuncture and herbal remedies.
Nourishing chi brings good health and
a long life.

BALANCING YIN AND YANG
IN THE BEDROOM

The bedroom is a place of rest where
yin should prevail, but not to excess.
Use calming yin colours for carpets and
curtains and balance it with yang in the
form of good lighting, which should not
be excessively bright. Avoid yang
energy in the form of live plants
and flowers.

BEDS, CANOPIES AND HEADBOARDS

The ideal bed is one that creates a feeling of refuge. Four-posters are excellent, and the addition of full canopies suggests safety and refuge. Headboards should be round and humped, resembling a tortoise. Avoid triangular, rectangular and wavy headboards.

TOILETS ATTACHED TO
BEDROOMS

Toilets and bathrooms attached to
bedrooms should always have their
doors kept closed. Hang a five-rod
wind chime inside the toilet and paint
the door red or white. Shades of blue
are considered inauspicious for toilets
as are flowers or plants.

SYMBOLS OF LONGEVITY

Longevity is a very important luck to
create. The Chinese believe that by
displaying symbols of longevity such as
the bamboo plant or Sau in the home,
the God of longevity, vibrant good
health energies are created which
ensure residents remain free of
fatal illnesses.

BAMBOO

The bamboo plant is regarded as highly auspicious, particularly the varieties with lots of little nodes. It is the most popular symbol of longevity and good health and should be planted in the east side of your garden. Alternatively a painting of bamboo can be hung on the east wall of the living room.

THE PEACH

Legend has it that it is the peach tree
which grows in the garden of the Queen
of the West that bears the fruit of
immortality, and today the peach is
another very popular symbol of
longevity. Eat plenty of peaches for
good health. Better still, display a
decorative peach tree in your
living room.

THE TORTOISE

This is a creature that brings good fortune to any household. It is another symbol of longevity and also a symbol of support and protection. Place a real or fake tortoise in the north of your house, preferably in the garden.

RITUALS OF PURIFICATION

Bedrooms should be symbolically purified on a regular basis using easy space clearing techniques. This is to ensure residents do not succumb to illnesses caused by stale energy. Air the room once a week by opening two sets of windows in the house, one inside the bedroom, and allow fresh air to blow into the room.

TRANSCENDENTAL
FENG SHUI

This uses visualization techniques
which supplement physical feng shui
cures. Close your eyes and relax, then
begin to create mental images of your
own inner chi annihilating the bad
energy that causes sickness. Visualize
blockages being dissolved inside as
well as outside you.

AN ABUNDANCE
OF LOVE

•

EXPERIENCE YOUR OWN
LOVE

Take a few minutes each day to tune
into yourself and focus on your being.
Observe your own feelings and
experience a sense of loving. Let this
awareness spread laterally outward
towards those who love and work
with you.

ATTRACTING LOVE INTO YOUR LIFE

Connecting to the loving self within you becomes easier each day and it quickly generates a positive energy around you that attracts more love into your life. If you want love, then make an effort to cultivate this kind of loving energy.

LOVE, MARRIAGE AND FAMILY

Since love, marriage and family
are all bound together in the Chinese
tradition, feng shui differentiates
sharply between marriage and having
a fling. Unless you are ready for
marriage it is better not to activate
marriage luck.

ACTIVATING MARRIAGE LUCK WITH FENG SHUI

Marriage is associated with the
southwest corner in feng shui, so
stimulating the elements of the
southwest energizes marriage luck.
Install a bright light or place crystals in
the southwest of the living room.

MANDARIN DUCKS

Mandarin ducks are wonderful symbols of marital togetherness. Place a painting of a pair of these ducks in your bedroom in the southwest corner, or a pair of ceramic, crystal or earthen mandarin ducks.

VISUALIZE YOUR FUTURE
PARTNER

Although very effective for attracting
marriage opportunities, activating the
southwest does not guarantee a perfect
spouse, nor that the match will be
either happy or long-lived. To create
a compatible match first analyse the
qualities you wish for in a partner and
then visualize the kind of mate
you want.

COMMITMENT PHOBICS

Unfortunately you cannot use feng shui to get a reluctant boyfriend or girlfriend to commit to marriage, or make someone who is not interested in you more so. You can, however, use feng shui to speed up the commitment process or to bring genuine marriage prospects into your life.

BALANCING YIN AND YANG FOR GOOD MARRIAGE LUCK

Balancing yin and yang energies in this
context means ensuring a good mix
of male and female energies. In feng
shui, opposites do not necessarily
attract and if the decor is excessively
feminine, chances of attracting a man's
permanent presence are diminished,
and vice versa.

SPECIAL ADVICE
FOR WOMEN

Feng shui is an ancient science geared
to the traditional values of making the
family patriarch rich, happy and
successful, and ensuring a plentiful
supply of concubines. In activating
prosperity luck in your home, be sure
you are not energizing your husband
for infidelity!

FLOWERS IN THE CONJUGAL BEDROOM

These signify the presence of many women in your life – like the old days when one man had many wives and concubines. Do not hang pictures of flowers or nude women in the bedroom.

MIRRORS IN THE CONJUGAL BEDROOM

The effect of mirrors or any reflective surfaces such as television screens facing the bed is that the marriage will be disturbed by the presence of a third party. They can also cause couples to be separated for long periods of time. Move them, cover them or enclose them within cupboards.

AN ABUNDANCE OF GOOD FAMILY LUCK

•

THE IMPORTANCE OF FAMILY

Family is the ultimate unit around which society and state evolves, and the traditional focal point of success and aspirations. Family wellbeing, names and descendants are therefore a significant feature in feng shui definitions of prosperity.

THE NORTHWEST: PLACE
OF THE PATRIARCH

This is the most important part of the
home since the luck of the patriarch, or
breadwinner, affects that of the whole
family. When the northwest corner of
the house is missing, luck associated
with career and income is missing and
the luck of the whole family is
seriously curtailed.

USING A MIRROR TO
CORRECT A MISSING
NORTHWEST CORNER

A wall mirror may be used to visually
'extend' a missing northwest corner if
the wall is part of the living or dining
room. Make sure the mirror covers the
entire wall, so the heads and feet of
residents are not cut off. Ensure the
mirror does not reflect the front door
or a toilet.

USING BRIGHT LIGHTS TO CORRECT A MISSING NORTHWEST CORNER

Regularize the shape of your home by installing a tall, bright light in the missing corner. The lamp should ideally be the height of the house.

ENHANCE THE NORTHWEST
WITH A WIND CHIME

A six-rod metal wind chime is one of
the best symbols to use for this corner
since it is in perfect harmony with the
element of the northwest. Hang it in
this part of the house or living room.
A metallic bell in the northwest is
another excellent energizer.

PREVENTING BAD FENG SHUI FOR THE BREADWINNER

A toilet, kitchen or storeroom in the northwest represents bad feng shui for the family. Hang a five-rod wind chime in toilets or kitchens in this corner to press down on negative energies. If a stove or cooker with a naked flame is placed here, reposition it immediately.

DO NOT ENERGIZE AN
AFFLICTED NORTHWEST
CORNER

If the northwest is where the toilet,
kitchen or storeroom are located, it is
inadvisable to energize the corner with
good fortune symbols. Your energizer
will simply become negatively affected
and the results will bring neither
abundance nor happiness.

THE SOUTHWEST: PLACE
OF THE MATRIARCH

The southwest is said to be the
receptacle of all good family luck for
the home. Placing a large ceramic,
terracotta or other clay urn or vase here
will allow a huge amount of chi to
accumulate and settle. Leave the urns
empty to attract and receive all the
good energy.

ENHANCING TECHNIQUES
FOR THE SOUTHWEST

A pile of boulders tied with red thread
in the southwest corner not only
safeguards against interior poison
arrows but reinforces the earth element
of the corner and energizes good
marriage luck. A painting of a
mountain or a cluster of quartz crystals
are excellent substitutes.

ACTIVATING FAMILY LUCK

The centre of the home represents the
family's relationship luck with one
another and is the ideal location for
family and dining rooms. Energize with
a crystal chandelier or a happy family
portrait. Family activities such as card
and board games, or watching
television create excellent
feng shui energy.

FENG SHUI FOR YOUR CHILDREN

From birth until the teenage years, children's bedrooms should ideally be on the east side of the home. Energize education luck by placing a small crystal globe in the northeast of the bedroom. It is not necessary to do anything else save to ensure there are no mirrors in the bedroom.

ACTIVATING FAMILY LUCK
IN THE NORTH

The element associated with the north
is water, so create harmony with blue
curtains and carpets. The north is also
the place of the black tortoise. A single
tortoise – real or decorative – in your
home ensures excellent good fortune.
An aquarium is another excellent
feature for the north.

ACTIVATING FAMILY LUCK
IN THE SOUTH

The element of the south is fire, so this
is an excellent place for a fireplace.
Keep this area well lit and paint red to
attract precious yang energy. Placing a
decorative bird here such as a peacock
or flamingo brings great good fortune.

ACTIVATING FAMILY LUCK
IN EAST AND SOUTHEAST

These are the places of the wood
element. Display flowers and plants in
these areas to symbolize growth. The
east is also the place of the green
dragon so placing a painting or ceramic
sculpture of a dragon in this corner
brings enormous good fortune.

ACTIVATING FAMILY LUCK
IN WEST AND NORTHWEST

Here the ruling colour is white or
metallic. Soft furnishings should
have a touch of gold to bring out the
auspicious energy of this corner.
The best energizers are the old coins
of the last dynasty of China.

ACTIVATING FAMILY LUCK IN NORTHEAST AND SOUTHWEST

The auspicious colours here are those that suggest the earth. Anything of the fire element is also auspicious since fire produces earth. Create a warm ambience with orange and ochre tones, and if the main door is located in either of these corners paint it red for good luck and harmony.

AN ABUNDANCE OF MATERIAL POSSESSIONS

•

THE UNIVERSE IS PLENTIFUL AND ABUNDANT

The belief that everyone is entitled to a lavish share, amplifies the abundance you create with feng shui. Material abundance is the easiest variety to achieve, but before you can become seriously wealthy you must believe you deserve to be rich.

MAKE SPACE FOR NEW POSSESSIONS

Unless you create space for them, new
possessions cannot come into your
home. Learn to give. It is not merely
outworn possessions and clutter that
you need to throw out. It is the mind
that needs to be transformed. The more
you give, the more you receive.

VISUALIZE EVERYTHING
YOU WANT

Keeping arrowana fish to create wealth
luck is a popular practice that works
for everyone, the only difference being
the differing amounts and kinds of
wealth it brings to different people.
Think carefully about what you want.
Focus your mind and give
your goals energy.

BUSINESS FENG SHUI
FOR PROFITS

Corporate profits are affected mainly by
the feng shui of the main door of the
office or building, and that of the chief
executive's office. Most bad feng shui
is due to the presence of killing chi
caused by other buildings. Take a
defensive approach.

GOOD FENG SHUI
FOR SHOPS

In general the busier the area, the more
plentiful the yang energy, and the
better the feng shui. Corner shops
usually have particularly good feng
shui. To enhance profits use mirrors to
line all your display walls. The mirror
should also reflect your cash register.

CHINESE COINS

Old Chinese coins are excellent money activators. Keep them in your wallet, taped onto important files, even on fax machines and computer monitors. Taping three coins tied with red thread onto the cash register, cash box or the invoice book generates higher income luck for businesses.

AN ABUNDANCE OF HAPPINESS

•

HAPPINESS – THE BLISS OF FEELING GOOD

I call happiness the feel good wealth. It describes the generous and good heart that is the best outcome of possessing abundance. This is the ultimate form of happiness because it engages the spiritual aspect latent within us all.

THE SOUL OF THE HOME

All homes have their own special brand
of energy. There are happy homes
which lift the spirit and sad homes
which create unease and tension.
Become aware of the feelings they
evoke and make mental notes about
layouts, energy flows, numbers of
openings, colours and shapes.

INVESTIGATE BACKGROUND HISTORY

Feng shui practitioners always investigate the background history of a home since old energies accumulated over many years take as long, if not longer, to dissipate. Be careful about land on which there was formerly a hospital, execution ground, abattoir or anything that connotes death or suffering.

SPATIAL HARMONY

Perhaps the most vital piece of the feng shui jigsaw is the way energy flows in any given room. When spatial harmony exists, the drift of energy will be slow, circuitous and auspicious, and the home will enjoy an abundance of good feeling.

FURNITURE
ARRANGEMENTS

Rooms should not be over furnished or
over decorated. There should be a
feeling of space and room for people to
move about comfortably. Try not to let
pieces of furniture jut out and create
sharp edges, and avoid L-shaped, U-
shaped and asymmetrical
arrangements.

SOFT FURNISHINGS

Ensure curtains do not smother the
room with either their texture or their
colour, and place plants in moderate
quantities. Paintings should blend with
the mood rather than create
discordant notes.

FLOWING WITH
AUSPICIOUS ENERGIES

Be creative, and adapt feng shui to suit
your own circumstances. Get just one
major thing correct – like the flow of
energy in your home – and you will
enjoy tremendous good fortune, and be
carried along a life of prosperity and
well-being. Be relaxed and never get
obsessive about feng shui.

The World of Feng Shui
online magazine is at:
http://www.wofs.com

Lillian Too's website is at:
http://www.lillian-too.com

Lillian Too's Jewellery site is at:
http//www.lilliantoojewellery.com

If you are interested in Buddhism,
please meet my lama at:
http//www.lamazopa.com